Impressum
Verlag: BABADADA GmbH, Nedderfeld 112 , 22529 Hamburg
Geschäftsführer / Verlagsleitung: Harald Hof
Druck: Books on Demand GmbH, In de Tarpen 42, 22848 Norderstedt

Imprint
Publisher: BABADADA GmbH, Nedderfeld 112 , 22529 Hamburg, Germany
Managing Director / Publishing direction: Harald Hof
Print: Books on Demand GmbH, In de Tarpen 42, 22848 Norderstedt

classroom
教室

divide
除

186/2

board
黑板

school yard
校園

teacher
老師

paper
紙

write
書寫

pen
筆

desk
辦公桌

ruler
直尺

book
書

pupil
學生

satchel

書包

pencil case

鉛筆盒

pencil

鉛筆

pencil sharpener

削鉛筆機

rubber

橡皮擦

drawing pad

畫板

drawing

圖畫

paintbrush

畫筆

paint box

顏料盒

scissors

剪刀

glue

膠水

exercise book

練習冊

homework

家庭作業

number

數字

add

加

subtract

減

multiply

乘

calculate

計算

letter

字母

alphabet

字母表

word

字

school - 學校

text

課文

read

讀

chalk

粉筆

lesson

上課

register

登記

exam

考試

certificate

證書

school uniform

校服

education

教育

encyclopedia

百科全書

university

大學

microscope

顯微鏡

map

地圖

paper bin

廢紙籃

hotel
飯店

hostel
青年旅社

bureau de change
外幣兌換處

suitcase
手提箱

car
汽車

language
語言

yes / no
是/否

Okay
好的

hello
您好

translator
翻譯人員

Thank you
謝謝

how much does ... cost?

......多少錢？

I do not understand

我不明白

problem

問題

Good evening!

晚上好！

Good morning!

早上好！

Good night!

晚安！

bye bye

再見

direction

方向

luggage

行李

bag

包

backpack

背包

guest

客人

room

房間

sleeping bag

睡袋

tent

帳篷

tourist information

旅行資訊

beach

海灘

credit card

信用卡

breakfast

早餐

lunch

午餐

dinner

晚餐

ticket

票

lift

電梯

stamp

郵票

border

邊界

customs

海關

embassy

大使館

visa

簽證

passport

護照

travel - 旅行

aeroplane
飛機

ship
船

fire engine
消防車

bus
公車

truck
卡車

motorboat
汽艇

car
汽車

bike
腳踏車

ferry

渡輪

boat

小船

motorbike

機車

police car

警車

racing car

賽車

rental car

租車

car sharing

拼車

breakdown truck

拖車

refuse truck

垃圾車

motor

馬達

fuel

汽油

petrol station

加油站

traffic sign

交通標識

traffic

交通

traffic jam

交通堵塞

car park

停車場

train station

火車站

tracks

軌道

train

火車

tram

路面電車

carriage

客車廂

helicopter

直升機

airport

機場

tower

塔

passenger

乘客

container

集裝箱

carton

紙板箱

cart

手推車

basket

籃子

take off / land

起飛/降落

city

城市

village

村莊

city centre

市中心

house

房子

cinema
電影院

advert
廣告

street light
路燈

CINEMA

street
街道

taxi
計程車

snack shop
小吃店

pedestrian
行人

pavement
人行道

zebra crossing
斑馬線

bin
垃圾箱

crossing
十字路口

traffic lights
紅綠燈

hut

小屋

flat

公寓

train station

火車站

town hall

市政廳

museum

博物館

school

學校

university

大學

bank

銀行

hospital

醫院

hotel

飯店

pharmacy

藥房

office

辦公室

book shop

書店

shop

商店

florist's

花店

supermarket

超市

market

市場

department store

百貨商店

fishmonger's

魚店

shopping centre

購物中心

harbour

海港

park

公園

bench

長凳

bridge

橋

stairs

樓梯

underground

捷運

tunnel

隧道

bus stop

公車站

bar

酒吧

restaurant

餐館

postbox

郵筒

road sign

路標

parking meter

停車計時器

zoo

動物園

swimming pool

游泳池

mosque

清真寺

farm
農場

pollution
污染

graveyard
墓地

church
教堂

playground
操場

temple
寺廟

landscape
地形

leaf
樹葉

signpost
指示牌

way
路

meadow
草地

stone
石頭

hiker
徒步旅行者

tree
樹

river
河

grass
草

flower
花

valley
峽谷

hill
丘陵

lake
湖

forest
森林

desert
沙漠

volcano
火山

castle
城堡

rainbow
彩虹

mushroom
蘑菇

palm tree
棕櫚樹

mosquito
蚊子

fly
蒼蠅

ant
螞蟻

bee
蜜蜂

spider
蜘蛛

beetle

甲蟲

frog

青蛙

squirrel

松鼠

hedgehog

刺蝟

hare

野兔

owl

貓頭鷹

bird

鳥

swan

天鵝

boar

野豬

deer

鹿

moose

麋鹿

dam

水壩

wind turbine

風力發電機

solar panel

太陽能電池板

climate

氣候

waiter
服務生

menu
菜譜

chair
椅子

soup
湯

pizza
披薩餅

cutlery
餐具

tablecloth
桌布

starter
前菜

main course
主菜

dessert
甜點

drinks
飲料

food
食物

bottle
瓶子

fast food

速食

street food

街邊小吃

teapot

茶壺

sugar bowl

糖盒

portion

一份飯菜

espresso machine

義式咖啡機

high chair

高腳椅

bill

帳單

tray

托盤

knife

刀

fork

餐叉

spoon

勺子

teaspoon

茶匙

serviette

餐巾

glass

玻璃杯

plate
....
碟子

soup plate
....
湯盤

saucer
....
碟子

sauce
....
醬

salt cellar
....
鹽瓶

pepper mill
....
胡椒研磨罐

vinegar
....
醋

oil
....
食用油

spices
....
調味料

ketchup
....
番茄醬

mustard
....
芥末

mayonnaise
....
美乃滋

special offer
特價

customer
顧客

FOR

dairy
乳製品

fruit
水果

trolley
購物車

butcher's

肉鋪

baker's

麵包店

weigh

稱重

vegetables

蔬菜

meat

肉

frozen food

冷凍食品

cold meat

冷盤

tinned food

罐頭食品

washing powder

洗衣粉

sweets

甜食

household products

日用品

cleaning products

清潔用品

salesperson

銷售員

till

收銀機

cashier

收銀員

shopping list

購物清單

opening hours

開放時間

wallet

錢包

credit card

信用卡

bag

袋子

plastic bag

塑膠袋

water

水

juice

果汁

milk

牛奶

coke

可樂

wine

紅酒

beer

啤酒

alcohol

酒

cocoa

可可

tea

茶

coffee

咖啡

espresso

義式濃縮咖啡

cappuccino

卡布奇諾

banana

香蕉

apple

蘋果

orange

柳丁

melon

西瓜

lemon

檸檬

carrot

胡蘿蔔

garlic

大蒜

bamboo

竹子

onion

洋蔥

mushroom

蘑菇

nuts

堅果

noodles

麵條

spaghetti

義大利麵

rice

米飯

salad

沙拉

chips

薯條

fried potatoes

炸馬鈴薯

pizza

披薩餅

hamburger

漢堡

sandwich

三明治

cutlet

炸豬排

ham

火腿

salami

義大利臘腸

sausage

香腸

chicken

雞肉

roast

烤肉

fish

魚

porridge oats

燕麥片

muesli

木斯里

cornflakes

玉米片

flour

麵粉

croissant

牛角麵包

bread roll

麵包捲

bread

麵包

toast

吐司

biscuits

餅乾

butter

奶油

curd

凝乳

cake

蛋糕

egg

蛋

fried egg

煎蛋

cheese

起司

ice cream

冰淇淋

sugar

糖

honey

蜂蜜

jam

果醬

chocolate spread

巧克力醬

curry

咖哩

farmhouse
農舍

straw bale
稻草捆

barn
糧倉

field
田野

horse
馬

trailer
拖車

foal
馬駒

tractor
拖拉機

donkey
驢

sheep
羊

lamb
羔羊

goat
山羊

cow
奶牛

calf
小牛

pig
豬

piglet
小豬

bull
公牛

goose

鵝

duck

鴨

chick

小雞

hen

母雞

cock

公雞

rat

鼠

cat

貓

mouse

老鼠

ox

牛

dog

狗

doghouse

狗屋

garden hose

花園澆水軟管

watering can

澆水壺

scythe

長柄大鐮刀

plough

犁

sickle
鐮刀

hoe
鋤頭

pitchfork
長柄草耙

axe
斧頭

wheelbarrow
獨輪手推車

trough
飼料槽

milk can
牛奶罐

sack
麻布袋

fence
柵欄

stable
馬廄

greenhouse
溫室

soil
土壤

seed
種子

fertilizer
肥料

combine harvester
聯合收割機

harvest

收割

harvest

收割

yams

地瓜

wheat

小麥

soy

大豆

potato

土豆

corn

玉米

rapeseed

油菜籽

fruit tree

果樹

cassava

樹薯

cereals

穀物

chimney
煙囪

roof
屋頂

drain pipe
落水管

window
窗戶

garage
車庫

doorbell
門鈴

door
門

rubbish bin
垃圾桶

letterbox
信箱

garden
花園

living room

客廳

bathroom

浴室

kitchen

廚房

bedroom

臥室

child's room

兒童房

dining room

餐廳

floor

地板

wall

牆壁

ceiling

天花板

cellar

地窖

sauna

三溫暖

balcony

陽臺

terrace

露臺

pool

游泳池

lawn mower

割草機

sheet

被單

bedspread

床罩

bed

床

broom

掃帚

bucket

水桶

switch

開關

wallpaper
壁紙

picture
相片

lamp
檯燈

shelf
擱架

cupboard
櫥櫃

television
電視

fireplace
壁爐

flower
花

cushion
墊子

sofa
沙發

vase
花瓶

remote control
遙控器

carpet

地毯

curtain

窗簾

table

餐桌

chair

椅子

rocking chair

搖椅

armchair

扶手椅

book

書

blanket

毯子

decoration

裝飾品

firewood

木柴

film

電影

hi-fi equipment

高傳真音響

key

鑰匙

newspaper

報紙

painting

油畫

poster

海報

radio

收音機

notepad

筆記本

hoover

吸塵器

cactus

仙人掌

candle

蠟燭

fridge
冰箱

microwave oven
微波爐

kitchen scales
廚房秤

toaster
烤麵包機

detergent
洗潔精

oven
烤箱

freezer
冰櫃

rubbish bin
垃圾桶

dishwasher
洗碗機

cooker

炊具

pot

鍋

cast-iron pot

鑄鐵鍋

wok / kadai

炒鍋

pan

平底鍋

kettle

水壺

steamer

蒸鍋

baking tray

烤盤

crockery

陶瓷鍋

mug

馬克杯

bowl

碗

chopsticks

筷子

ladle

長柄勺

spatula

鏟子

whisk

攪拌器

strainer

濾網

sieve

篩子

grater

磨碎機

mortar

研缽

barbecue

燒烤

open fire

明火

chopping board
菜板

rolling pin
擀麵杖

corkscrew
開瓶器

can
罐子

can opener
開罐器

pot holder
隔熱手套

sink
水槽

brush
刷子

sponge
海綿

blender
攪拌機

deep freezer
冷藏箱

baby bottle
奶瓶

tap
水龍頭

heating
供暖裝置

shower
淋浴

towel
毛巾

bubble bath
泡沫浴

shower curtain
浴簾

bathtub
浴缸

glass
玻璃杯

washing machine
洗衣機

tiles
瓷磚

tap
水龍頭

potty
便壺

sink
水槽

toilet
廁所

squat toilet
蹲便器

bidet
坐浴器

urinal
小便斗

toilet paper
廁紙

toilet brush
馬桶刷

toothbrush

牙刷

toothpaste

牙膏

dental floss

牙線

wash

洗

handheld shower

手持式蓮蓬頭

douche

沖洗器

basin

洗臉盆

back brush

洗背刷

soap

肥皂

shower gel

沐浴露

shampoo

洗髮乳

flannel

法蘭絨

drain

排水

cream

乳霜

deodorant

除臭劑

mirror

鏡子

hand mirror

手鏡

razor

刮鬍刀

shaving foam

刮鬍泡沫

aftershave

鬚後水

comb

梳子

brush

刷子

hair dryer

吹風機

hairspray

噴髮定型劑

makeup

化妝品

lipstick

唇膏

nail varnish

指甲油

cotton wool

化妝棉

nail scissors

指甲剪

perfume

香水

washbag

洗漱包

stool

凳子

weighing scale

計重秤

bathrobe

浴袍

rubber gloves

橡膠手套

tampon

衛生棉條

sanitary towel

衛生棉

chemical toilet

化學廁所

alarm clock
鬧鐘

cuddly toy
毛絨玩具

toy car
玩具車

doll's house
玩具屋

present
禮物

rattle
撥浪鼓

balloon

氣球

bed

床

pram

嬰兒車

deck of cards

撲克牌

jigsaw

拼圖

comic

漫畫

lego bricks

樂高積木

building blocks

積木玩具

action figure

公仔

romper suit

嬰兒服

Frisbee

飛盤

mobile

床鈴玩具

board game

棋盤遊戲

dice

骰子

model train set

火車模型

dummy

安撫奶嘴

party

派對

picture book

繪本

ball

球

doll

洋娃娃

play

玩

sandpit

沙坑

swing

鞦韆

toys

玩具

video game console

電玩遊戲

tricycle

三輪車

teddy bear

泰迪熊

wardrobe

衣櫃

clothing

衣服

socks

襪子

stockings

長襪

tights

緊身褲

scarf
圍巾

belt
皮帶

umbrella
雨傘

t-shirt
T恤

trainers
運動鞋

boots
靴子

slippers
拖鞋

sandals

涼鞋

shoes

鞋

rubber boots

雨靴

underpants

內褲

bra

胸罩

vest

背心

body

身體

trousers

褲子

jeans

牛仔褲

skirt

短裙

blouse

女式襯衫

shirt

襯衫

pullover

套頭衫

hoodie

連帽上衣

blazer

西裝夾克

jacket

夾克

coat

外套

raincoat

雨衣

costume

套裝

dress

連衣裙

wedding dress

婚紗

suit

西裝

nightgown

睡袍

pyjamas

睡衣

sari

莎麗

headscarf

頭巾

turban

包頭巾

burqa

波卡

kaftan

卡夫坦

abaya

(阿拉伯式)長袍

swimsuit

泳衣

trunks

男式泳褲

shorts

短褲

tracksuit

運動服

apron

圍裙

gloves

手套

button

鈕扣

glasses

眼鏡

bracelet

手鏈

necklace

項鍊

ring

戒指

earring

耳環

cap

便帽

coat hanger

衣架

hat

帽子

tie

領帶

zipper

拉鍊

helmet

安全帽

braces

背帶

school uniform

校服

uniform

制服

bib
圍兜

dummy
安撫奶嘴

nappy
尿布

server
伺服器

filing cabinet
檔案櫃

printer
印表機

paper
紙

monitor
螢幕

mouse
滑鼠

desk
辦公桌

folder
資料夾

keyboard
鍵盤

chair
椅子

paper bin
廢紙簍

computer
電腦

coffee mug
咖啡杯

calculator
計算機

internet
網際網路

laptop

筆記型電腦

letter

信件

message

簡訊

mobile

行動電話

network

網路

photocopier

影印機

software

軟體

telephone

電話

plug socket

插座

fax machine

傳真機

form

表格

document

檔案

buy

買

pay

付錢

trade

交易

money

現金

dollar

美元

euro

歐元

yen

日元

rouble

盧布

Swiss franc

瑞士法郎

renminbi yuan

人民幣

rupee

盧比

cashpoint

提款處

bureau de change

外幣兌換處

gold

金

silver

銀

oil

石油

energy

能源

price

價格

contract

合約

tax

稅金

stock

股票

work

工作

employee

職員

employer

老闆

factory

工廠

shop

商店

police officer
警官

fireman
消防員

cook
廚師

doctor
醫師

pilot
飛行員

gardener

園丁

carpenter

木匠

seamstress

裁縫

judge

法官

chemist

化學家

actor

演員

bus driver

公車司機

taxi driver

計程車司機

fisherman

漁夫

cleaning lady

清洗女工

roofer

屋頂工

waiter

服務生

hunter

獵人

painter

畫家

baker

麵包師

electrician

電工

builder

建築工人

engineer

工程師

butcher

屠夫

plumber

水管工

postman

郵差

soldier

士兵

architect

建築師

cashier

收銀員

florist

花農

hairdresser

理髮師

conductor

售票員

mechanic

機械技師

captain

船長

dentist

牙醫

scientist

科學家

rabbi

拉比

imam

伊瑪目

monk

和尚

clergyman

牧師

hammer
鐵錘

pliers
鉗子

screwdriver
螺絲起子

spanner
扳手

torch
手電筒

digger
挖掘機

toolbox
工具箱

ladder
梯子

saw
鋸子

nails
釘子

drill
鑽機

repair
修

shovel
鏟子

Damn!
糟糕！

dustpan
畚箕

paint pot
油漆桶

screws
螺絲

musical instruments
樂器

loudspeaker
揚聲器

drum kit
打擊樂器

guitar
吉他

double bass
低音提琴

trumpet
小號

piano

鋼琴

violin

小提琴

bass

貝斯

timpani

定音鼓

drums

鼓

keyboard

電子琴

saxophone

薩克斯風

flute

長笛

microphone

麥克風

tiger
老虎

entrance
入口

cage
籠子

zebra
斑馬

animal feed
動物飼料

panda
熊貓

animals

動物

elephant

大象

kangaroo

袋鼠

rhino

犀牛

gorilla

大猩猩

bear

熊

camel

駱駝

ostrich

鴕鳥

lion

獅子

monkey

猴子

flamingo

紅鶴

parrot

鸚鵡

polar bear

北極熊

penguin

企鵝

shark

鯊魚

peacock

孔雀

snake

蛇

crocodile

鱷魚

zookeeper

動物園管理員

seal

海豹

jaguar

美洲豹

pony

矮種馬

leopard

豹

hippo

河馬

giraffe

長頸鹿

eagle

老鷹

boar

野豬

fish

魚

turtle

龜

walrus

海象

fox

狐狸

gazelle

羚羊

American football
橄欖球

cycling
騎腳踏車

tennis
網球

basketball
籃球

swimming
游泳

boxing
拳擊

ice hockey
冰球

football
....
美式足球

badminton
羽毛球

athletics
田徑

handball
....
手球

skiing
滑雪

polo
馬球

jump
跳

laugh
笑

hug
擁抱

walk
走路

sing
唱

dream
做夢

pray
祈禱

kiss
親吻

write
書寫

draw
畫

show
展示

push
推

give
給

take
拿

have
有

do
做

be
當

stand
站

run
跑

pull
拉

throw
丟

fall
摔倒

lie
躺

wait
等待

carry
攜帶

sit
坐

get dressed
穿衣

sleep
睡覺

wake up
醒來

look at
看

cry
哭

stroke
擊

comb
梳頭

talk
交談

understand
明白

ask
問

listen
聽

drink
喝

eat
吃

tidy up
清理

love
愛

cook
做飯

drive
開車

fly
飛

activities - 活動

sail

航行

calculate

計算

read

讀

learn

學習

work

工作

marry

結婚

sew

縫

brush teeth

刷牙

kill

殺

smoke

抽菸

send

寄

grandmother
祖母

grandfather
祖父

father
父親

mother
母親

baby
嬰兒

daughter
女兒

son
兒子

guest

客人

aunt

阿姨

uncle

叔叔

brother

兄弟

sister

姐妹

forehead
前額

eye
眼睛

shoulder
肩膀

finger
手指

face
臉

chin
下巴

hand
手

breast
乳房

leg
腿

arm
手臂

baby
嬰兒

man
男人

woman
女人

girl
女孩

boy
男孩

head
頭

back

背部

belly

肚子

belly button

肚臍

toe

腳趾

heel

腳後跟

bone

骨頭

hip

臀部

knee

膝蓋

elbow

手肘

nose

鼻子

bottom

屁股

skin

皮膚

cheek

臉頰

ear

耳朵

lip

嘴唇

body - 身體

mouth

嘴

tooth

牙齒

tongue

舌頭

brain

腦

heart

心臟

muscle

肌肉

lung

肺

liver

肝臟

stomach

胃

kidneys

腎臟

sex

性交

condom

保險套

ovum

卵子

semen

精子

pregnancy

懷孕

menstruation

月事

vagina

陰道

penis

陰莖

eyebrow

眉毛

hair

頭髮

neck

脖子

body - 身體

hospital
醫院

ambulance
急救車

wheelchair
輪椅

fracture
骨折

doctor

醫師

emergency room

急診室

nurse

護理師

emergency

緊急情形

unconscious

昏迷

pain

痛

injury

受傷

bleeding

出血

heart attack

心臟病發作

stroke

中風

allergy

過敏

cough

咳嗽

fever

發燒

flu

流感

diarrhoea

腹瀉

headache

頭痛

cancer

癌症

diabetes

糖尿病

surgeon

外科醫師

scalpel

手術刀

operation

手術

CT

電腦斷層掃描

x-ray

X光

ultrasound

超音波

face mask

口罩

disease

疾病

waiting room

候診室

crutch

拐杖

plaster

石膏

bandage

繃帶

injection

注射

stethoscope

聽診器

stretcher

擔架

clinical thermometer

體溫計

birth

出生

overweight

超重

hearing aid

助聽器

disinfectant

消毒液

infection

感染

virus

病毒

HIV / AIDS

愛滋病

medicine

藥物

vaccination

接種疫苗

tablets

藥片

pill

藥丸

emergency call

急救電話

blood pressure monitor

血壓計

sick / healthy

生病/健康

Help!

救命！

alarm

警報

assault

突擊

attack

攻擊

danger

危險

emergency exit

緊急出口

Fire!

失火了！

fire extinguisher

滅火器

accident

意外

first-aid kit

急救箱

SOS

呼救訊號

police

員警

Europe

歐洲

North America

北美洲

South America

南美洲

Africa

非洲

Asia

亞洲

Australia

澳洲

Atlantic

大西洋

Pacific

太平洋

Indian Ocean

印度洋

Antarctic Ocean

南冰洋

Arctic Ocean

北冰洋

North Pole

北極

South Pole

南極

Antarctica

南極洲

Earth

地球

land

陸地

sea

海

island

島

nation

國家

state

州

clock face

錶盤

hour hand

時針

minute hand

分針

second hand

秒針

What time is it?

現在幾點？

day

天

time

時間

now

現在

digital watch

電子錶

minute

分

hour

時

Monday 週一 MO
Wednesday 週三 W
Friday 週五 FR
TU
TH
SA
Tuesday 週二
Saturday 週六
Thursday 週四
SO
Sunday 週日

yesterday

昨天

today

今天

tomorrow

明天

morning

早晨

noon

中午

evening

晚上

MO	TU	WE	TH	FR	SA	SU
1	2	3	4	5	6	7
8	9	10	11	12	13	14
15	16	17	18	19	20	21
22	23	24	25	26	27	28
29	30	31	1	2	3	4

business days

工作日

MO	TU	WE	TH	FR	SA	SU
1	2	3	4	5	6	7
8	9	10	11	12	13	14
15	16	17	18	19	20	21
22	23	24	25	26	27	28
29	30	31	1	2	3	4

weekend

週末

rain
雨

rainbow
▶ 彩虹

wind
風

snow
雪

spring
春

summer
夏

autumn
▶ 秋

winter
冬

weather forecast
....
天氣預告

thermometer
....
溫度計

sunshine
....
陽光

cloud
....
雲

fog
....
霧

humidity
....
潮濕

lightning

閃電

thunder

打雷

storm

風暴

hail

冰雹

monsoon

季風

flood

洪水

ice

冰

January

一月

February

二月

March

三月

April

四月

May

五月

June

六月

July

七月

August

八月

year - 年

September
....
九月

October
....
十月

November
....
十一月

December
....
十二月

shapes
形狀

circle
....
圓形

square
....
正方形

rectangle
....
長方形

triangle
....
三角形

sphere
....
球體

cube
....
立方體

white

白

yellow

黃

orange

橙

pink

粉

red

紅

purple

紫

blue

藍

green

綠

brown

棕

grey

灰

black

黑

a lot / a little

很多/少許

angry / calm

生氣/平靜

beautiful / ugly

美/醜

beginning / end

首/尾

big / small

大/小

bright / dark

明/暗

brother / sister

兄弟/姐妹

clean / dirty

乾淨/骯髒

complete / incomplete

完整/缺失

day / night

白天/晚上

dead / alive

死/生

wide / narrow

寬/窄

edible / inedible

可食用/非食用

evil / nice

邪惡/善良

excited / bored

興奮/無聊

fat / thin

胖/瘦

first / last

第一/最後

friend / enemy

朋友/敵人

full / empty

滿/空

hard / soft

硬/軟

heavy / light

重/輕

hunger / thirst

餓/渴

sick / healthy

生病/健康

illegal / legal

非法/合法

intelligent / stupid

聰明/愚笨

left / right

左/右

near / far

近/遠

new / used

新/舊

nothing / something

沒有/有些

old / young

老/幼

on / off

開/關

open / closed

打開/闔上

quiet / loud

安靜/吵鬧

rich / poor

富/窮

right / wrong

對/錯

rough / smooth

粗糙/光滑

sad / happy

傷心/高興

short / long

短/長

slow / fast

慢/快

wet / dry

濕/乾

warm / cool

溫暖/涼爽

war / peace

戰爭/和平

opposites - 反義詞

0

zero

零

1

one

一

2

two

二

3

three

三

4

four

四

5

five

五

6

six

六

7

seven

七

8

eight

八

9

nine

九

10

ten

十

11

eleven

十一

12

twelve

十二

13

thirteen

十三

14

fourteen

十四

15

fifteen

十五

16

sixteen

十六

17

seventeen

十七

18

eighteen

十八

19

nineteen

十九

20

twenty

二十

100

hundred

百

1.000

thousand

千

1.000.000

million

百萬

languages
語言

English
英語

American English
美式英語

Mandarin Chinese
普通話

Hindi
印地語

Spanish
西班牙語

French
法語

Arabic
阿拉伯語

Russian
俄語

Portuguese
葡萄牙語

Bengali
孟加拉語

German
德語

Japanese
日語

I

我

you

你

he / she / it

他/她/它

we

我們

you

你們

they

他們

who?

誰？

what?

什麼？

how?

如何？

where?

何處？

when?

何時？

name

名字

behind

後面

in

裡面

in front of

前面

over

上方

on

上面

under

下麵

beside

旁邊

between

中間

place

地點